Immigration to the United States

Polish Immigrants

W. Scott Ingram

Robert Asher, Ph.D., General Editor

☑®
Facts On File, Inc.

Immigration to the United States: Polish Immigrants

Facts On File, Inc.
132 West 31st Street
New York NY 10001

Library of Congress Cataloging-in-Publication Data

Ingram, Scott.
    Polish immigrants / W. Scott Ingram, Robert Asher.
        p. cm. – (Immigration to the United States)
    Includes bibliographical references and index.
    ISBN 0-8160-5686-2
    1. Polish Americans–History–Juvenile literature. 2. Immigrants–United States–
History–Juvenile literature. 3. Polish Americans–Juvenile literature. I. Asher, Robert.
II. Title. III. Series.
    E184.P7I54 2004
    973'.049185–dc22

                                                                                2004017852

Facts On File books are available at special discounts when purchased in bulk quantities for businesses, associations, institutions, or sales promotions. Please call our Special Sales Department in New York at (212) 967-8800 or (800) 322-8755.

You can find Facts On File on the World Wide Web at http://www.factsonfile.com

Cover design by Cathy Rincon
A Creative Media Applications Production
Interior design: Fabia Wargin & Lúis Leon
Editor: Laura Walsh
Copy editor: Laurie Lieb
Photo researcher: Jennifer Bright

Photo Credits:
p. 1 © AP Photo/Gino Domenico; p. 4 © Sandy Felsenthal/CORBIS; p. 11 © Bettmann/CORBIS; p. 15 © Bettmann/CORBIS; p. 17 © Bettmann/CORBIS; p. 19 © Bettmann/CORBIS; p. 20 © Hulton Archive/Getty Images; p. 21 © Hulton Archive/Getty Images; p. 27 © Bettmann/CORBIS; p. 29 © Bettmann/CORBIS; p. 33 © Minnesota Historical Society/CORBIS; p. 34 © CORBIS; p. 37 Courtesy Fabia Wargin; p. 40 © Library of Congress; p. 44 © Scheufler Collection/CORBIS; p. 47 © Bettmann/CORBIS; p. 49 © CORBIS; p. 51 © AP Photo; p. 53 Courtesy Jennifer Bright; p. 57 © AP Photo; p. 61 © CORBIS; p. 64 © Hulton Archive/Getty Images; p. 69 © Bettmann/CORBIS; p. 71 © Annie Griffiths Belt/CORBIS; p. 73 © AP Photo; p. 78 © Bettmann/CORBIS; p. 80 Courtesy Hellada Gallery, Long Beach, Ca. ; p. 84 © Bettmann/CORBIS

Printed in the United States of America

VH PKG 10 9 8 7 6 5 4 3 2 1

This book is printed on acid-free paper.

Previous page: *Pulaski Day parades, named in honor of Revolutionary War hero Kazimierz Pulaski, are one way Polish Americans celebrate their heritage. These marchers took part in New York City's parade in October 1997.*

Contents

A Nation
of Immigrants

Robert Asher, Ph.D.

Left: *This view of
Milwaukee Avenue
in Chicago, taken
in 1995, shows one
of the vibrant
Polish communi-
ties in that city,
which has a huge
Polish-American
population.*

Human beings have always moved from one place to another. Sometimes they have sought territory with more food or better economic conditions. Sometimes they have moved to escape poverty or been forced to flee from invaders who have taken over their territory. When people leave one country or region to settle in another, their movement is called emigration. When people come into a new country or region to settle, it is called immigration. The new arrivals are called immigrants.

People move from their home country to settle in a new land for two underlying reasons. The first reason is that negative conditions in their native land push them to leave. These are called "push factors." People are pushed to emigrate from their native land or region by such things as poverty, religious persecution, or political oppression.

The second reason that people emigrate is that positive conditions in the new country pull them to the new land. These are called "pull factors." People immigrate to new countries seeking opportunities that do not exist in their native country. Push and pull factors often work together. People leave poor conditions in one country seeking better conditions in another.

Sometimes people are forced to flee their homeland because of extreme hardship, war, or oppression. These immigrants to new lands are called refugees. During times of war or famine, large groups of refugees may immigrate to new countries in search of better conditions. Refugees have been on the move from the earliest recorded history. Even today, groups of refugees are forced to move from one country to another.

Pulled to America

For hundreds of years, people have been pulled to America seeking freedom and economic opportunity. America has always been a land of immigrants. The original settlers of America emigrated from Asia thousands of years ago. These first Americans were probably following animal herds in search of better hunting grounds. They migrated to America across a land bridge that connected the west coast of North America with Asia. As time passed, they spread throughout North and South America and established complex societies and cultures.

Beginning in the 1500s, a new group of immigrants came to America from Europe. The first European immigrants to America were volunteer sailors and soldiers who were promised rewards for their labor. Once settlements were established, small numbers of immigrants from Spain, Portugal, France, Holland, and England began to arrive. Some were rich, but most were poor. Most of these emigrants had to pay for the expensive ocean voyage from Europe to the Western Hemisphere by promising to work for four to seven years. They were called indentured servants. These emigrants were pushed out of Europe by religious persecution, high land prices, and poverty. They were pulled to America by reports of cheap, fertile land and by the promise of more religious freedom than they had in their homelands.

Many immigrants who arrived in America, however, did not come by choice. Convicts were forcibly transported from England to work in the American colonies. In addition, thousands of African men, women, and children were kidnapped in Africa and forced onto slave ships. They were transported to America and forced to work for European masters. While voluntary emigrants had some choice of which territory they would move to, involuntary immigrants had no choice at all. Slaves were forced to immigrate to America from the 1500s until about 1840. For voluntary immigrants, two things influenced where they settled once they arrived in the United States. First, immigrants usually settled where there were jobs. Second, they often settled in the same places as immigrants who had come before them, especially those who were relatives or who had come from the same village or town in their homeland. This is called chain migration. Immigrants felt more comfortable living among people whose language they understood and whom they might have known in the "old country."

Immigrants often came to America with particular skills that they had learned in their native countries. These included occupations such as carpentry, butchering, jewelry making, metal machining, and farming. Immigrants settled in places where they could find jobs using these skills.

In addition to skills, immigrant groups brought their languages, religions, and customs with them to the new land. Each of these many cultures has made unique contributions to American life. Each group has added to the multicultural society that is America today.

Waves of Immigration

Many immigrant groups came to America in waves. In the early 1800s, economic conditions in Europe were growing harsh. Famine in Ireland led to a massive push of emigration of Irish men and women to the United States. A similar number of

German farmers and urban workers migrated to America. They were attracted by high wages, a growing number of jobs, and low land prices. Starting in 1880, huge numbers of people in southern and eastern Europe, including Italians, Russians, Poles, and Greeks, were facing rising populations and poor economies. To escape these conditions, they chose to immigrate to the United States. In the first 10 years of the 20th century, immigration from Europe was in the millions each year, with a peak of 8 million immigrants in 1910. In the 1930s, thousands of Jewish immigrants fled religious persecution in Nazi Germany and came to America.

Becoming a Legal Immigrant

There were few limits on the number of immigrants that could come to America until 1924. That year, Congress limited immigration to the United States to only 100,000 per year. In 1965, the number of immigrants allowed into the United States each year was raised from 100,000 to 290,000. In 1986, Congress further relaxed immigration rules, especially for immigrants from Cuba and Haiti. The new law allowed 1.5 million legal immigrants to enter the United States in 1990. Since then, more than half a million people have legally immigrated to the United States each year.

Not everyone who wants to immigrate to the United States is allowed to do so. The number of people from other countries who may immigrate to America is determined by a federal law called the Immigration and Naturalization Act (INA). This law was first passed in 1952. It has been amended (changed) many times since then.

Following the terrorist attacks on the World Trade Center in New York City and the Pentagon in Washington, D.C., in 2001, Congress made significant changes in the INA. One important change was to make the agency that administers laws concerning immigrants and other people entering the United States part of the Department of Homeland Security (DHS). The DHS is responsible for protecting the United States from attacks by terrorists. The new immigration agency is called the Citizenship and Immigration Service (CIS). It replaced the previous agency, which was called the Immigration and Naturalization Service (INS).

When noncitizens enter the United States, they must obtain official permission from the government to stay in the country. This permission is called a visa. Visas are issued by the CIS for a specific time period. In order to remain in the country permanently, an immigrant must obtain a permanent resident visa, also called a green card. This document allows a person to live, work, and study in the United States for an unlimited amount of time.

To qualify for a green card, an immigrant must have a sponsor. In most cases, a sponsor is a member of the immigrant's family who is a U.S. citizen or holds a green card. The government sets an annual limit of 226,000 on the number of family members who may be sponsored for permanent residence. In addition, no more than 25,650 immigrants may come from any one country.

In addition to family members, there are two other main avenues to obtaining a green card. A person may be sponsored by a U.S. employer or may enter the Green Card Lottery. An employer may sponsor a person who has unique work qualifications. The Green Card Lottery randomly selects 50,000 winners each year to receive green cards. Applicants for the lottery may be from any country from which immigration is allowed by U.S. law.

However, a green card does not grant an immigrant U.S. citizenship. Many immigrants have chosen to become citizens of the United States. Legal immigrants who have lived in the United States for at least five years and who meet other requirements may apply to become naturalized citizens. Once these immigrants qualify for citizenship, they become full-fledged citizens and have all the rights, privileges, and obligations of other U.S. citizens.

Even with these newer laws, there are always more people who want to immigrate to the United States than are allowed by law. As a result, some people choose to come to the United States illegally. Illegal immigrants do not have permission from the U.S. government to enter the country. Since 1980, the number of illegal immigrants entering the United States, especially from Central and South America, has increased greatly. These illegal immigrants are pushed by poverty in their homelands and pulled by the hope of a better life in the United States. Illegal immigration cannot be exactly measured, but it is believed that between 1 million and 3 million illegal immigrants enter the United States each year.

This series, Immigration to the United States, describes the history of the immigrant groups that have come to the United States. Some came because of the pull of America and the hope of a better life. Others were pushed out of their homelands. Still others were forced to immigrate as slaves. Whatever the reasons for their arrival, each group has a unique story and has made a unique contribution to the American way of life. ❧

Right: Photographed around 1910, two young Polish women prepare to leave the immigration center at Ellis Island in New York Harbor to begin new lives in the United States.

Polish Immigration

Seeking a Better Life

Today, more than 9 million people of Polish descent live in the United States, making Polish Americans the seventh-largest ethnic group in the country. Most of the Poles who came to the United States arrived between 1870 and 1920, a period when millions of immigrants from Europe came to America. During that period, it is estimated that more than 2 million people of Polish descent entered the United States.

It is difficult to estimate the number of Poles who came to the United States during that period because at that time there was no actual country of Poland as it is known today. Polish immigrants were identified in the U.S. Census, the official count of the population, as people who spoke the Polish language and followed the Roman Catholic faith. But some Poles did not fit that description because they followed the Jewish faith.

Early Kingdom

For several centuries before the 1700s, Poland was a large European kingdom that was widely admired for its political, religious, and intellectual freedoms. Poland eventually changed from an independent kingdom to a land of colonies ruled by other European countries, mostly because of its location. In fact, much of Poland's history has been guided by its geography and its environment.

Poland is located in eastern Europe, with a northern border along the Baltic Sea. The country of Lithuania lies to the northeast, Belarus is on the eastern border, and Ukraine lies to the southeast. To the south are the Czech Republic and Slovakia. Germany lies to the west.

Poland is a land of great natural resources. Southwest Poland has enormous coal deposits and eastern Poland is a region of thick forests. More than three-fourths of Poland, however, is flat farmland intersected by the Vistula, Odra, Warta, and Bug rivers. Poland's capital, Warsaw, lies in the center of these fertile plains.

Throughout European history, the plains of Poland have been a battleground for opposing armies as well as a breadbasket that provided food for conquering countries.

Earliest Arrivals

The first Polish immigrants to the United States arrived in Jamestown, Virginia, in 1608. In the early 1700s, several hundred Poles who converted from Catholicism to the Quaker faith came to the Pennsylvania colony that had been founded by Quaker leader William Penn.

The first whole community made up of Polish Americans was founded in 1854 on the plains southeast of San Antonio, Texas. The settlement was named Panna Maria, which means "Virgin Mary" in Polish. The first major wave of Polish immigration brought about 400,000 Poles to the United States by 1860. Most of these Polish immigrants came to the United States alone or in small family groups. They settled in American cities of the Northeast and Midwest.

In the final decades of the 19th century, Poles joined the flood of European immigrants entering the United Stated from eastern and southern Europe. Among these immigrants were more than 2 million people of Polish descent who came to the United States from various nations of Europe, including the areas of their homeland under foreign control.

Tragedy in the 20th Century

For Poles and for Poland, the 20th century was a time of tragedy that began in 1914, with the outbreak of World War I in Europe. Poland's location between Germany and Austria to the west and Russia to the east made it a battleground during the war.

When the war ended in November 1918, Poland became an independent nation for the first time in 123 years. Over the next decade, as Poles attempted to rebuild their own country, few of them immigrated to the United States. Restrictions on immigration to the United States also contributed to the decrease in the number of Polish immigrants.

In 1939, an even greater tragedy struck Poland than the disaster of World War I. After just 21 years of independence, Poland again fell to a conquering power. On September 1, the armies of Nazi Germany, under orders from dictator Adolf Hitler, invaded Poland. This event triggered World War II, perhaps the most devastating period in the history of Poland.

In 1945, the armies of the Soviet Union drove the Nazis from Poland. The liberation, however, left war-torn Poland under the control of the Soviet Union and its leader, Joseph Stalin, a dictator who was in many ways as brutal as Hitler. Because the United States was engaged in a rivalry with the Soviet Union called the cold war, over the next decade a number of laws were passed that allowed more people seeking freedom from Soviet control to come to the United States, including Poles.

Poland remained under the economic and political control of the Soviet Union until 1980, when strikes by Polish shipyard workers forced changes in the government. Over the first half of that decade, Poland's military rulers attempted to regain political power through violence and intimidation, causing a number of Poles to flee to the United States.

In August 1989, the Soviet Union and all of the European governments it controlled collapsed. Poland became an independent nation once again. Even so, Poland suffered from economic problems throughout the 1990s. As a result of the difficulties in Poland, many Poles continued to immigrate to the United States.

The United States and Poland are close allies. Polish troops were stationed in Iraq and supported U.S. troops during the Iraq War, which began in 2003. The relations that were first formed between Poles and colonial Americans have grown stronger over several centuries. Polish Americans, both citizens and new arrivals, have become an important part of the fabric of the United States. 🏵

Opposite: Among those who worked to build the Jamestown Colony in Virginia were a number of Poles, who arrived in 1608. Some early settlers are shown in this illustration.

Chapter One

Early Immigration

The First Polish Americans

Poles in Jamestown

Polish immigration to the North American continent began long before there was a country known as the United States. It began at a time when most Americans were Native Americans, and there were very few white people anywhere on the continent. The first Poles to arrive in North America came to Jamestown, Virginia, in 1608. The first permanent English settlement in North America had been established there a year earlier.

These first Polish immigrants quickly proved to be valuable members of the small settlement at Jamestown. Among them were skilled workers hired by the English to make pitch, tar, and resins used to waterproof wooden ships, a key part of England's growth as an empire. In addition, the Poles made glass, which became important in the Jamestown economy.

Poland

*Jamestown settlers were probably happy to see Poles arrive in 1608.
Some of them were skilled workers who helped the colony thrive. In this
illustration, settlers greet a ship bringing more settlers to the colony.*

The Polish immigrants were considered so important to
Jamestown that the settlement's financial backers, the Virginia
Company of London, made arrangements for the workers to
train others. Yet, as important as the Poles were to Jamestown,
because they were Polish they were denied one basic right that
all of Jamestown's English male residents had: the right to vote.

In 1619, Polish workers refused to work until they were
granted the right to vote. The records of the Jamestown colony
note that the protest was successful. An entry from July 21, 1619,
states: "Upon some dispute of the Polonians [Poles] resident in
Virginia, it was agreed that they shall be enfranchised [given the

right to vote], and made as free as any inhabitant there whatsoever." (At the time, no woman, no matter what nationality she was, had the right to vote. Therefore, when the Poles in Jamestown were given this right in 1619, it applied only to men.)

Events in Poland

It's a Fact!

More than 150 years after Polish workers in Jamestown protested for the right to vote, American colonists would fight to be "free" from Great Britain. It was the Poles, however, who had staged the first political protest in the American colonies.

By the time the first Poles arrived in North America, the country of Poland was more than 500 years old. In 1609, a year after the first Polonia arrived in America, Poland fought the first in a long series of wars against invading armies from Sweden across the Baltic Sea, Turkey from the south, and Russia from the east. For more than a century, Poland was both a target of conquering armies and a battleground for opposing kingdoms. To the Poles, this time is known as the "Deluge," a long period of death and destruction.

By the late 1600s, Poland was almost entirely under the control of Russia. But the wars were not over. Poland was in constant turmoil because of its location at the crossroads of Europe. It became a pawn in the struggle for power of the three great powers in that region of Europe at the time: Russia, Prussia, and Austria.

In 1762, Catherine the Great became the empress of Russia. In 1764, she picked Stanislaw Poniatowski to rule Poland. Catherine assumed that Stanislaw, as he was known, would rule the country as she wished. But Stanislaw turned against Catherine and began to push for Poland to become an independent kingdom.

A young Catherine the Great is shown in this painting from 1748,
14 years before she became empress of Russia.

As a result, a revolt by Polish nobles arose against Catherine in 1772. The revolt was successful at first, and the rulers of Prussia and Austria, whose empires bordered Poland, grew concerned. They quickly joined forces with Catherine's army to defeat the Poles. The Poles' revolt not only failed, it resulted in Poland's being partitioned, or split, into three separate colonies, each ruled by one of the three powers.

Poles in the American Revolution

Many Poles who fought unsuccessfully for Poland's independence in 1772 felt a strong bond with the American colonists who were fighting for independence from Great Britain. At the beginning of the American Revolution in 1775, the American inventor and statesman Benjamin Franklin was sent to Paris to seek financial and military support from France. In Paris, Franklin met a number of Polish exiles who supported the American cause.

During the American Revolution (1775–1781), more than 100 Poles came to America to fight for American independence. Among these fighters were two of the most honored military leaders of the Revolution: General Tadeusz Kosciuszko and General Kazimierz Pulaski.

Kosciuszko was the first important military officer from Europe to offer his services to the Americans. He was a skilled construction engineer who specialized in the design of forts, bridges, and defensive fortifications. In the key American victory at Saratoga, New York, in 1777, Kosciuszko designed the fortifications that protected American troops from the British. In 1778, he designed the fort overlooking the Hudson River at West Point, New York, which is today the location of the U.S. Military Academy.

General Tadeusz Kosciuszko is shown in a portrait from 1790. Kosciuszko came from Poland to help the Americans in the Revolutionary War.

Pulaski, a cavalry officer in Poland, came to the American colonies in 1777 and immediately took command of the disorganized American horse-mounted troops. Although the 30-year-old officer did not speak English, he immediately won the support of General George Washington at the Battle of Brandywine in Delaware. Although the Americans were defeated at Brandywine, Pulaski's fast-moving unit held back a British force that had almost

Kazimierz Pulaski, was fatally wounded at Savannah, Georgia, in October 1779, as shown in this illustration.

surrounded the Americans and would have cut off their retreat.

For two years, Pulaski worked to build an American cavalry that could scout and report on British movements. In 1779, Pulaski was fatally wounded leading a cavalry charge at the battle of Savannah, Georgia. A hero of the American Revolution, Pulaski is known as the "father of the American cavalry."

Vincinanki

★★★

One of the most distinctive decorations found in many homes of Polish Americans, both past and present, are paper cutouts called *vincinanki* (vee-chee-nan-ki). The practice began in Polish farming regions during the mid-1800s as a way to decorate walls, beams, doorways, and windows, especially during the Easter holiday.

To make *vincinanki*, Polish women used hand-colored paper that they folded in half. With scissors, they cut out the shapes of roosters, peacocks, and other animals, as well as uniquely shaped flowers and trees. They glued these shapes to white backgrounds to create country scenes.

The First Polish Settlement

T he revolts in Poland that led to its partition in 1772 would rise and be crushed twice more until, in 1794, Poland was divided for the third and final time by Russia, Prussia, and Austria. The country known as Poland disappeared from the map.

The final partition, or division, of Poland pushed the first large wave of Poles to the United States. Meanwhile, the success of the new United States government, a democracy, pulled Poles who hated the foreign domination of their homeland. Records of the number of Poles who immigrated to the United States in the late 18th and early 19th century, however, are not accurate because there was no recognized country of Poland. Most Poles who came to the United States during that time were listed as Germans or Austrians.

It's a Fact!

Tadeusz Kosciuszko returned to Poland after the American Revolution and led the third and final revolt against the foreign powers in his native country, in 1794. Kosciuszko did not have the success in Poland that he had in America, however. His Polish forces were defeated by the larger Russian army.

In 1830, a short-lived revolt broke out in Russian-controlled Poland. The revolt was crushed, and about 1,000 Poles from that region came to the United States. With financial assistance from Americans who were sympathetic to the Polish struggle for independence, these immigrants settled in New York City. There, this small community of Poles formed the first Polish organization to assist future immigrants, the Association of Poles in America. Polish-American organizations such as this also collected funds to help pay the costs of Poles who wished to immigrate. In 1849, a Pole in Warsaw wrote a letter to the Association of Poles in America asking for money to pay for a journey to the United States:

> *I want to go to America. But I have no money. I have nothing but the ten fingers of my hands, a wife, and nine children. I have no work at all, although I am strong and healthy and only forty-five years old. I have been to many cities and towns in Poland. Nowhere could I earn money. I wish to work. But what can I do. I will not steal. I beg you to accept me for a journey to America.*

From the very first years of Polish immigration, all newcomers considered it a duty to write letters to family and local acquaintances back in Poland. This was impossible for many immigrants who could not read or write, so they turned to local Polish organizations for help. These letters gave a great deal of practical advice

Polish Americans in the Civil War

At the outbreak of the American Civil War in 1861 a number of Poles enlisted in the Union, or northern, forces to fight against the Confederate forces of the South. Among the most distinguished military officers of the war was Polish immigrant Joseph Karge, who had been an officer in the Prussian army before coming to the United States. Karge led the New Jersey Cavalry, a unit of soldiers on horseback. He was the only Union cavalryman to defeat the legendary Confederate general Nathan Bedford Forrest.

Another important Pole who contributed to the Union cause was Wlodzimierz Krzyzanowski, who rose to the rank of general. He commanded troops in the Polish Legion, an immigrant unit, in battles at Bull Run and Cross Keys in Virginia and at Gettysburg, Pennsylvania. Appointed by President Abraham Lincoln, Krzyzanowski was said to have been denied a promotion because members of Congress could not pronounce or spell his name.

to those about to emigrate to the United States about living and working conditions in America. Although some letters wildly exaggerated the possibilities for success in the United States, this communication link was important in bringing Poles to America.

As a result of these communications, most Polish immigrants who came to the United States during the first half of the 19th century settled in cities, such as New York City, where large numbers of immigrants from other countries had also settled. In the late 1840s, however, conditions for Poles in the Prussian-controlled region of Silesia resulted in the establishment of the first large Polish settlement outside of a major U.S. city.

Prussian Silesia, which is today in southwestern Poland, was populated largely by Polish peasants who had kept their ties to their conquered homeland by speaking Polish, observing Polish customs, and following their faith, which was mainly Roman Catholic. In the late 1840s and early 1850s, epidemics of disease killed thousands of Poles in Silesia. Floods destroyed crops and food shortages led to widespread starvation. In addition, Prussia was engaged in a war during those years, and many Poles in Silesia were forced to fight in the Prussian army.

In 1851, a Polish Roman Catholic priest, Father Leopold Moczygemba, was sent to the town of New Braunfels, Texas, by church authorities. He was assigned to a church founded by German immigrants who had settled in the plains of south Texas. Moczygemba soon realized that the wide-open lands of the state would provide farmland for his fellow Poles from Silesia. He wrote letters back to his family and friends in Silesia, urging them to come to Texas.

In December 1854, a boat carrying 150 Poles arrived in the Texas port of Galveston. Walking or riding in wagons, the Poles traveled inland for three weeks before meeting Moczygemba. The priest had gathered enough money to buy a piece of land near the city of San Antonio.

Polish Names

One of the most distinctive aspects of Polish identity is the surnames, or last names, by which Poles are known. Polish surnames are easily identified by their final letters, or suffixes. The most common suffixes in Polish surnames are -ski, -wicz, and -czyk.

The suffix -ski means "of the" or "from the." A name ending in -ski may indicate that a family has a close connection with a place or with a certain occupation. A family whose ancestors originated in the city of Warsaw, for example, might have the last name Warsawski. A surname such as Pierkarski is based on the Polish word for "baker"—*piekar*. Thus, this surname might mean "of the baker's family" or "from the place of bakers."

The suffix -wicz, pronounced "wits," means "son of." Thus, the last name Jakubowicz means "son of Jacob."

The suffix -czyk, pronounced "chik," can also mean "son of" and also means "little." A surname such as Kowalczyk is based on the Polish word for "blacksmith"—*kowal*. Thus, Kowalczyk means "son of the blacksmith" or "little blacksmith."

The Poles named their new community Panna Maria, which means "Virgin Mary" in Polish. Throughout the winter of 1855, the settlers built wooden houses and barns. They also built a Catholic church in which Moczygemba held services. In the spring, they planted corn, the main food of both people and livestock in Texas. Unfortunately for these first settlers, they faced challenges right away.

In the summer of 1855, a plague of grasshoppers invaded the corn field and nearly destroyed the crop. That was followed by a 14-month drought. The only food the settlers had for more than a year was wild rabbits and deer hunted by the town residents. Further grasshopper invasions occurred throughout the 1850s, and some settlers moved away. Despite these hardships, however, most of the Polish immigrants remained in Panna

Maria. By 1869, a stone school had been built for the settlement's children.

News of the settlement at Panna Maria led to the establishment of similar Polish farming communities in Wisconsin and Michigan. Although these towns were small, they established a path of immigration of Poles to the Midwest.

After the Civil War (1861–1865), the U.S. economy became more industrialized. As a result, most Poles who came to the United States from 1860 on went to rapidly growing cities. Large Polish communities formed in Buffalo, New York, and in the eastern Pennsylvania cities of Scranton and Wilkes-Barre. Further west, industrial centers such as Pittsburgh, Pennsylvania; Cleveland and Toledo, Ohio; and Chicago, Illinois, developed large Polish communities. By the 1870s, in fact, Chicago was known as the "American Warsaw," with a population of more than 40,000 Poles.

Opposite: *Many Polish Jews who immigrated to the United States during the last half of the 19th century left their homeland to escape religious persecution. This Polish grandfather gives his grandson religious instruction at home in Biala, Poland, a city that was ruled by Austria-Hungary until after World War I.*

Chapter Two

The First
Great Wave

Poles Leave the Homeland

A Change in Plans

Many of the Poles who came to the United States during the first half of the 19th century did not plan to remain in America. The dream of an independent Poland was shared by many Polish immigrants, and most planned to return to their homeland when Austria, Prussia, and Russia gave up control of their colonies there. During the first five decades of the century, there were a number of revolts by Poles in all three regions of Poland under foreign control. None of the revolts was successful, however, and each failure made the lives of the Polish people worse, as the foreign rulers tightened their grip.

For this reason, many Poles who came to the United States during the second half of the 19th century had little hope of returning to an independent Poland. Most were primarily concerned with their own basic survival and cared less about political freedom for their homeland.

Prussia to Germany

The next large emigration of Poles to the United States occurred as a result of turmoil in the area of Poland controlled by Prussia. Much of this turmoil was caused by the rise to power of a Prussian minister, or political leader, named Otto von Bismarck. When Bismarck became prime minister of Prussia in 1862, he started various programs that eventually took land away from Polish peasant farmers and gave it to wealthy nobles and business owners.

Along with these land policies, Bismarck, who believed that ethnic Germans were superior to other groups, created what he called a "culture war." This policy was aimed at weakening the power of the Catholic Church, which he felt threatened the power of the German empire. The government closed Catholic schools, imprisoned Polish church officials, and forbade Poles from practicing their religion.

Bismarck's rigid ideas and his belief in German superiority also affected another religious and ethnic group in Poland—the Jews. In 1869, a follower of Bismarck named William Marr founded the League for Anti-Semitism. (Anti-Semitism is the hatred of and discrimination against Jews.) Marr promoted the idea that Jews were inferior to Germans in every way. This popular opinion made life unbearable for Poland's Jews, who were forced to live apart from others and had few rights.

The actions and prejudice of Prussian prime minister Otto von Bismarck, who came to power in 1862, forced many Poles in German-controlled areas to flee to the United States. This photograph of von Bismarck was taken in 1894.

This combination of actions by Bismarck and his followers led thousands of Poles, both Jewish and Catholic, to leave German Poland. The first wave of Polish immigrants from that area began to arrive in the United States in the 1860s. Over the next three decades, more than 400,000 Poles from German-controlled regions immigrated to the United States.

In general, German Poles were better educated than Poles living in Austrian- or Russian-controlled areas of Poland. These immigrants felt an obligation to form organizations to assist other Poles who planned to follow them to the United States. These organizations were called mutual aid societies.

Community Markets

Many Polish immigrants were people from farming villages who were used to small-town life. Arriving in a city where most people spoke English, a language that both sounded and looked unfamiliar, was a frightening experience for most newcomers. For this reason, Polish-American markets became one of the most popular gathering places for immigrants. These small stores provided more than food. They helped immigrants stay connected to their culture.

In these stores, immigrants could buy kielbasa (Polish sausage) and pierogi (dough stuffed with potato, cheese, or cabbage). For the Easter holiday, they could buy butter in the shape of a lamb, a Polish tradition. For Christmas, Polish shopkeepers sold ducks, whose blood was used to make *czerina* (duck soup). The stores also had the butter, flour, eggs, and raisins needed to make *placek* (coffee cake), which was served on Christmas morning. Many larger stores also sold dried mushrooms, books, toys, cloth, and other items imported from Polish lands.

In addition to traditional foods, the markets served as meeting places for the exchange of news from the homeland or from other Polish communities. While the local church was the traditional center of Polish life, the markets were often the first step in establishing a Polish neighborhood in an American city.

Polish immigrant Anton Schermann was one of the first to organize a mutual aid society. Schermann came to Chicago from Prussia in the 1860s. After working for several years as a laborer, he opened a grocery store that became a gathering place for new Polish arrivals. Schermann set aside a room in his store to hold meetings of what became known as the St. Stanizlaus Society, a group that raised funds to build a Catholic church and bring over clergy to hold services.

For more than 40 years, Schermann advised and helped start other organizations that served the growing Polish immigrant community in Chicago. In this role, he oversaw a community treasury that was established to help immigrant families through crises such as sickness, accidents, or death. He also helped individual Poles make travel arrangements and created a system that assisted Poles in communicating with friends and acquaintances in Europe. His store also served as a community labor office where Poles looking for work gathered to be hired by local bosses. Schermann's efforts are credited with having "brought over" more than 40,000 Poles to Chicago in the last half of the 19th century. Many Polish communities in the northern and midwestern United States arose due to similar efforts by German Poles.

Russian and Austrian Poles

Between about 1860 and 1890, the majority of Poles coming to the United States came from German lands. The efforts of these immigrants to bring fellow Poles to United States pulled immigrants from Polish lands ruled by Austria and Russia beginning in the 1880s. Like the German Poles, many of these Poles suffered political and religious persecution. In some areas of Russian-controlled Poland, Poles were prohibited from speaking their language. A person could be imprisoned for speaking Polish in church.

Besides political or religious persecution, however, Poles in Austrian- and Russian-held areas suffered extreme economic hardship. In these mostly rural regions, people depended on farming to survive. For Poles, land ownership was their only security. With land they could grow food to eat and perhaps enough to sell in a village market.

But as Bismarck had done in Germany in the 1860s, both Austria and Russia started policies in the 1880s that took land from small farmers and placed it under the control of wealthy nobles. Suddenly, peasants who had farmed land for generations were forced to leave their family farms. Unlike in the German areas, however, there were no large industrial cities to which these peasants could go for work. In the Austrian-controlled area of Poland, called Galicia, the period beginning about 1880 is known as the era of "Galician misery."

Because of the communication system between Poles in the United States and those in Europe, however, many of these peasants, who were mostly uneducated, were attracted by the possibility of work in America. Word that laborers in the United States earned between 90 cents and a dollar a day—10 times their current wage—persuaded millions of peasants to make the long journey to America.

It's a Fact!

The era of Galician misery occurred at a time when the population of Poles in the area grew by more than 20 percent. Thus, at a time when peasants were being forced out of their traditional way of life, the population density—the number of people per square mile—was the highest of any rural area in Europe.

Journey and Settlement

P oles were a major part of the enormous wave of immigrants that started coming to the United States from eastern and southern Europe in the 1880s. Most Polish immigrants left their homeland by traveling across the Atlantic Ocean to New York City. This journey remained basically unchanged from 1880 to 1914.

Polish and Russian immigrants were photographed on the deck of their ship to America around 1905.

A Polish immigrant carries his trunk as he leaves the ship
President Grant *upon arriving at Ellis Island in 1907.*

Poles generally sailed by steamship from one of two German ports, Bremerhaven or Hamburg. A ticket from either of these ports to New York City cost about $10, an amount equal to more than three months' wages in the region they were leaving. (In today's money, this is roughly $189.) For this price, immigrants were usually confined below decks for most of the trip, in the travel class known as steerage. Conditions were dreadful during these trips. An investigative reporter who made a trip across the Atlantic in steerage wrote: "How can a steerage passenger remember that he is a human being when he must first pick the worms from his food . . . and eat in a stuffy, stinking bunk, or in the hot . . . atmosphere of a compartment where 150 men sleep."

Despite these conditions, more than 2 million Poles made the journey to the United States between 1880 and 1914. Observing Poles in steerage during a voyage in 1896, American author Edward Steiner wrote: "Poles . . . are among the most industrious [hardworking] and patient people who come to our shores. Even on board ship they are the most patient passengers, for hardships are not new to them." For these desperate people, a week or two in steerage would be forgotten once they were able to begin new lives.

Polish Dancing

One of the richest traditions Polish immigrants have brought to the United States is their love of folk dancing. Dances have always played an important part in Polish festivals in both Poland and the United States. Some dances, such as the *oberek*, are done in groups, somewhat like American square dancing. The *krakowiak* is a group dance that is well known for its rapid pace and its stamping, kicking, and leaping. More formal dances, such as the mazurka and the *kujawiak*, are traditionally done by couples.

Without a doubt, the most famous Polish dance is the polka. The polka—the name means "Polish woman"—was brought to the United States by Polish immigrants in the huge wave of immigration during the late 19th century. With its quick, two-step sliding motion, the dance was well-suited to a wide variety of American immigrant musical styles. Thus, the traditional violin-played polkas from Poland were eventually played by bands that included accordion, drums, clarinets, and other instruments. By the mid-20th century, polka music included jazz, Latin, and country-and-western sounds.

Today, polka festivals are a common event in Polish-American communities. Some cities with large Polish populations have regular radio and television shows featuring polka music and dancing.

All immigrants who landed in New York City after 1892 were detained at the Immigration Center on Ellis Island in New York Harbor. Even before the steamships landed, however, American officials boarded the ships. Few Poles who arrived in this large wave of immigrants were refused admission to the United States for any reason. Records show that fewer than 1 percent of all Poles were denied entry between 1892 and 1905.

The overall acceptance of Polish immigrants was mostly a result of the strong community organizations that had been established by the first arrivals. By the 1890s, Poles could count on any of dozens of Polish-American welfare and immigration societies in the Polonia—the Polish community—for help in finding work and shelter.

In general, Poles who came to the United States also had relatives, friends, or other acquaintances waiting for them in the United States. Unlike many immigrants who arrived with little idea of where to go, "virtually all" Poles, according to a 1900 report, were able to give immigration officials a definite destination and the names of people they were joining in the United States. By the beginning of the 20th century, the massive migration of Poles from Europe was well under way.

It's a Fact!

An immigrant usually purchased a steamship ticket to the United States with money raised from selling personal belongings or livestock. In some cases, money was sent from Polish-American organizations or other contacts in the United States.

Opposite: *The Koscielski family, a Polish-American family from Chicago, was photographed in 1930. The little girl on the right is wearing a traditional Polish costume.*

Chapter Three

The New
Century

Polish Immigrants in America

More Opportunity

Most of the immigrants who came to the United States between 1880 and 1914 came as the result of the country's enormous industrial expansion. The manufacture of steel used in steamships and especially railroads, for example, created huge numbers of jobs in mines and factories.

Like many other immigrants, Poles were pulled to the United States by stories of high pay and excellent living conditions. But the reality, for many immigrants, was disappointing. One Polish immigrant wrote back to acquaintances in Europe to complain about his experience: "What people from America write to Poland is [false]; there is not a word of truth. For in America Poles work like cattle. Where a dog does not want to sit, there a Pole is made to sit, and the poor wretch works because he wants to eat."

It was true that pay was higher in the United States than in Poland. But immigrants still had to cope with homesickness and prejudice. Some wondered if they had made the right choice by leaving their homeland.

From Rural to Urban

This letter reflects what was generally an uncomfortable period of transition for Poles. While most Polish immigrants were persuaded to come to the United States by other Poles, there was little waiting for them except other Poles who were settled in crowded, ramshackle city neighborhoods. Most Polish immigrants were forced to take jobs at the lowest level of the economic scale in the worst urban areas of the time.

Adding to the difficult adjustment was the fact that most Poles had lived in rural settings before coming to the United

States. Their lives were centered on farming. Yet fewer than one-tenth of Polish immigrants in the peak years of immigration were able to become farmers once they reached the United States. Farming required large amounts of land, which poor Polish immigrants could not afford to buy. Some German Poles did settle in farming areas of the Midwest, mostly in Minnesota and Wisconsin. A few Poles arriving at the start of the 20th century settled in farming areas of eastern Long Island, New York, and in the Connecticut River valley region of New England.

Most Polish immigrants, however, were never able to leave their backbreaking jobs in northern U.S. cities. According to a 1907 study, more than 80 percent of Polish immigrants were unskilled laborers. Men were usually employed in the lowest-paying positions in coal mines, meatpacking factories, steel mills, and garment-manufacturing sweatshops. (These workplaces were called sweatshops because they were hot, unventilated, crowded, and uncomfortable.) The pay averaged about $1.50 for a 12- to 14-hour workday. The average yearly income for a Polish immigrant was slightly more than $300 per year (about $6,000 in today's money, which is well below the poverty line). Although these wages were more than Poles could earn in their homeland, they were not enough to ensure a comfortable life in America.

As they adapted from rural to city life in a new country, Poles often managed to live similarly to the way they had in Europe. Economic struggles they had faced in their homeland taught them how to get by on very little. Most Polish-American families in the cities, for example, had small vegetable gardens in which they raised foods such as cabbage and potatoes. If they were fortunate to have a home with a small yard, Polish-American families often kept goats or chickens unless prohibited by city laws. The immigrants' diet was simple. In addition to their homegrown vegetables, Poles ate cheap cuts of pork, sausage, smoked fish, and dark bread.

These children were photographed playing in the streets of a Polish community in Chicago in 1903. The business behind them, Polska Stacya, is a Polish saloon.

The frugality of Poles allowed them to save a great deal of money. Many Poles were able to save enough money to purchase property. In their traditional culture, owning property was the basic measure of wealth. By 1901, nearly 30 percent of all Poles in the United States owned some real estate. In some cities, these homes became known as "Polish flats"—small one-story buildings that were often remodeled in order to provide living quarters for friends, relatives, or boarders, who paid the owners to live there.

Many Poles also used their savings to help their relatives back in Poland. A study in 1907 found that Polish boarders in Chicago, for example, were sending back almost two-thirds of their $25-a-month salaries to their families in Poland. In 1910, it was estimated that Poles in the United States had sent about $40 million back to Austrian and Russian Poland.

An Immigrant Family

One example of the hard lives of Polish immigrants was recorded in a 1986 interview with 80-year-old Victor Kobylarz. Kobylarz described the daily life of his mother, Aniela Nieradtka Kobylarz, who was born in Austrian-controlled Poland in 1882. She immigrated to the United States with her husband Franciszek (Frank) Kobylarz in 1901 and settled in Passaic, New Jersey. Aniela worked in a silk factory for eight cents an hour and her husband worked as a glassblower. By 1914, the family had saved enough to buy a farm in Tioga, New York.

While many Polish families were large, averaging about six children, few families were larger than the Kobylarz family. There were 18 children, and a 19th child was adopted. Victor Kobylarz described how his mother kept food on the table:

> *Every other day she used 25 pounds of flour. She had a great, big wood stove so she could put 12 loaves of bread in the oven at one time. And this went on winter and summer, every other day. Then Saturday, she made what we called* paczki *(dough-nuts). . . . Every Sunday morning, she made six or eight pies. She never measured anything. When you ask[ed] about a recipe, "How much? Half a cup?" she said, "Gaszka tego, gaszka tego." In Polish a handful is a* gaszka. *So it was "a handful of this . . . a handful of that."*

> *We ate a lot of potatoes and cabbage and raised twenty or more pigs. All winter long she was canning pork, canning beef. We had no freezers, no refrigerators. I'd say she put up a thousand jars of meat every winter.*

> *She had 18 kids before we got electricity and she got a washing machine. Do you realize how many thousand diapers she scrubbed on . . . washboards?*

Aniela Kobylarz did more than cook, clean, take care of the house, and raise 18 children, according to her son. She kept boarders as well, a common practice among Polish immigrant families in the early part of the 20th century. She also did farm chores in the barn and fields.

Kobylarz said his mother's Roman Catholic faith was extremely important to her. "She didn't have to pray to enter heaven; she worked her way to heaven without praying," he added. Aniela Kobylarz died in 1986 at the age of 104.

Polish Jews

In 1880, there were fewer than 250,000 Jews in the United States. Most of them had immigrated during colonial times or from German states in the first half of the 19th century. Between 1881 and 1924, more than 4 million Jews arrived in the United States. These immigrants came mainly from eastern Europe, including what is today Poland.

Jews, like other immigrants, were pulled to the United States by the opportunity to improve their standard of living and pushed out of their homelands by terrible economic conditions. But unlike most other immigrants, Jews were often forced out of their homes. The population of Jews in Polish areas increased dramatically in the 1800s, from about 1.5 million to 7 million. This growth led to an increase in the persecution of Jews. Some Poles and other non-Jewish ethnic groups came to believe that Jews were "taking over" banks, lands, and other important resources. By the early 1880s, the poison of anti-Semitism had made the situation for most eastern European Jews extremely perilous.

Since immigration records did not record religion, it is difficult for historians to know exactly how many Jews came from the three controlled areas of Poland. Almost all Jews who emigrated from Polish areas spoke Polish as well as the language of their controlling powers—German, Austrian, or Russian. The only distinguishing factor in records of the time is that most Jewish immigrants listed their main language as Yiddish—a language derived from Hebrew, German, and eastern European languages.

Holiday Traditions

Many traditional Polish holiday traditions are closely connected to the Roman Catholic faith. Traditions and faith are especially significant during the Christmas and Easter holidays.

Polish families begin their Christmas celebration on Christmas Eve. One beloved custom is the sharing of *oplatki*, a wafer known as the "bread of love." The thin bread is cut into narrow strips and placed on the dining table as a centerpiece for the *Wigilia*, the meal served on Christmas Eve. With the family gathered around the table, the *oplatki* is passed around and everyone takes a small strip. They exchange good wishes and eat the bread. Tradition holds that all bad thoughts must be replaced by goodwill at this time.

The *Wigilia* begins when the first star can be seen in the sky on Christmas Eve. An extra place is set for Jesus, for a stranger who may appear, or for an absent family member. After the meal, gifts are exchanged, and Christmas carols called *koleny* are sung. At midnight, everyone attends the Christmas Mass, called *pasterka*. Christmas Day is for sleeping late and visiting friends.

Easter is also a strong tradition among Polish Americans. The well-known custom of decorating and coloring hard-boiled eggs, called *pysanky* in Polish, began centuries ago in Poland. Easter food is less traditional than Christmas food and often includes meat. The meal is eaten after Mass on Easter morning. Traditionally, the centerpiece of every table is a *baranek*, or butter molded into the shape of a lamb. This serves as a symbol of Jesus.

Once Jewish immigrants arrived in the United States, they were free to establish their own synagogues (Jewish houses of worship and communal centers) and communities, just as other immigrant groups did. The largest number of them settled in the Northeast, especially New York City. United by their common language, Jews from all parts of eastern Europe, including Poland, formed strong, supportive communities free from the persecution they had suffered in their homelands.

A Polish rabbi, or Jewish religious leader, was photographed in the late 1860s or early 1870s in Krakow, Poland.

Religion in Immigrant Life

Although neighborhood markets and Polish assistance organizations were important elements of immigrant life, the Roman Catholic faith was the center of the Polish community. Immigrants were quick to establish churches virtually everywhere they settled.

As the population of Polish immigrants continued to grow, the number of churches did as well. In 1870, for example, Poles had established 17 Roman Catholic churches in the United States. By 1910, there were more than 500 such Polish Roman Catholic churches.

The rapid growth of Polish Catholic churches led to conflict between Poles and other Catholic immigrant groups, primarily the Irish. By the early 1900s, Irish Americans were beginning to move into the middle class of American society. As a result, they had greater influence in the selection of religious leaders for all American Catholics, including the Poles.

Poles were fiercely loyal to the idea of Polish clergy (religious leaders) serving Polish communities in the United States. They resented what many bitterly called "The Holy Irish Church." This attitude was expressed by Father Francis Hodur, a Polish priest who wrote in the early 1900s, "The Polish people should control all churches built by them. They should choose their own pastors. If a church community speaks Polish, the priest must speak Polish too."

In 1904, this conflict led Poles to break away from the American Catholic Church and form the Polish National Catholic Church (PNCC). Within several years, the PNCC had more than 30 churches and more than 30,000 followers. Although this was only a fraction of the millions of Polish Catholics in the United States, concern over the break between Catholics of different ethnic backgrounds reached the highest levels of the Catholic Church in Rome, Italy. In response, Roman Catholic leaders appointed a Pole, Father Paul Rhode, as the first Polish-American bishop in 1908.

Anti-Immigrant Prejudice

While many Americans grudgingly accepted immigrants such as the Poles, others were hostile toward them. By contrast, some immigrants from northern and western Europe, especially those who spoke English, felt accepted almost immediately upon their arrival in the United States. Poles and other immigrant groups from southern and eastern Europe, meanwhile, often felt unwelcome.

Beginning in the 1890s, American Protestants, who were generally the wealthiest and best-educated Americans, were alarmed at the waves of Roman Catholic, Greek Orthodox, and Jewish immigrants entering the country. A strong prejudice arose against immigrants whom many Protestants considered "inferior," especially immigrants from eastern and southern Europe.

In 1894, a group of young men from Harvard University in Cambridge, Massachusetts, founded the Immigration Restriction League (IRL). The IRL became very influential with the public as well as with leaders of the U.S. government. To keep out "undesirables," the IRL proposed a law requiring all immigrants to pass a literacy test, proving that they could read and write their native language. The test was created specifically to discriminate against Poles and other immigrants, who had never gone to school and usually did not know how to read or write.

Although the IRL literacy test was approved by Congress several times, three different presidents vetoed, or refused to sign, the act because it was unfair.

The Pan-American Assassination

By 1900, the city of Buffalo, New York, had a Polish population of about 70,000 people. Polish Americans made up nearly 20 percent of the population of the entire city. Because of its location near Canada, Buffalo was selected as the site of the 1901 Pan-American Exposition, a special gathering, like a fair, at which countries in North and South America could highlight their cultures. Years of planning went into the huge event.

*An artist at the Buffalo Pan-American Exposition made this illustra-
tion of Leon Czolgosz's shooting of President William McKinley on
September 6, 1901. The president died of his wounds on September 14.*

At that time, most of Buffalo's Poles were manual laborers.
In fact, Poles did much of the work in the construction of the
exposition buildings and the railroads that would bring visitors
to the grounds. But what should have been a proud example of
the work done by Polish immigrants in the United States was
marred by tragedy, for Polish Americans and the United States
as a whole.

On September 6, 1901, President William McKinley appeared at the fair and was shaking hands with local citizens. Suddenly, 28-year-old Leon Czolgosz, a son of Polish immigrants, pulled out a pistol and shot McKinley twice. Czolgosz was an anarchist, a person who is against any form of government and anyone in a position of authority, such as the president of the United States. The president died from his wounds eight days later.

The fact that Czolgosz was a Polish American created feelings of shame and anger among Buffalo's Polonia. A planned parade and celebration of Polish Heritage Day at the exposition was canceled by community leaders. Buffalo's Polish-language newspaper had a headline that read DISGRACE TO THE NAME. The article began:

> *Poles of Buffalo are deeply incensed [angered] against the . . . assassin of the President, as they feel he has dragged the Polish fair name in the mire. . . . Czolgosz should not call himself a Pole, and the Buffalo colony fears his [name] may bring unjust [accusations] on its members.*

Czolgosz was found guilty of murder and executed on October 29, 1901. Despite the fact that he was an American citizen by birth, his actions and his "un-American" last name fueled the anti-immigration movement in the United States. The assassination of the president was a key argument used by anti-immigration organizations for closing the doors of the United States to immigrants.

Opposite: *Members of a working-class Polish-American family are pictured on their porch in Mauch Chunk (later renamed Jim Thorpe), Pennsylvania. Many Polish immigrants who lived in coal mining towns in Pennsylvania suffered from poor economic conditions created by the Great Depression.*

Chapter Four

War and Depression

1914–1941

A Dream of Independence

According to the U.S. Census, in 1900 there were about 2 million people of Polish descent living in the United States. From 1901 until 1914, about 100,000 Poles immigrated to the United States per year.

No matter what area of foreign-dominated Poland these immigrants came from, most shared the same dream of an independent nation of Poland. By the first decade of the 20th century, the drive for a free Poland was once again a key unifying factor among the many Polish-American organizations that arose in immigrant communities. During that time, a number of Polish immigrants returned to Russian and Austrian Poland to organize support for Polish independence.

World War I

In June 1914, the assassination of the heir to the throne of Austria set in motion a series of events that led to war and, eventually, to a free Poland. The Austrian heir, Archduke Franz Ferdinand, was shot by Gavrilo Princip, a native of the eastern European country of Serbia. Like Poland, Serbia had long been under Austrian control. Princip believed that the assassination would help bring about independence for Serbia.

Instead, the assassination led to the invasion of Serbia by Austrian troops and, very quickly, to a war involving most of the nations of Europe and eventually the United States. The three nations that controlled Poland were deeply involved in the war. Both Russia and Austria, who were fighting against each other, offered the Polish people their independence in exchange for Polish military support. Later, American president

Woodrow Wilson called for the establishment of an "independent Polish State" once the Central Powers, including Austria and Germany, were defeated.

President Woodrow Wilson supported the establishment of an independent Poland.

Meanwhile, Poland's location between Russia and its main foe, Germany, meant that a great deal of fighting took place there. When the war ended in the autumn of 1918 with the defeat of Austria and Germany, much of Europe was in ruins. In all, more than 10 million soldiers as well as 10 million civilians had died over four years. The toll was also high in Poland. A total of 2 million Polish troops had fought with the armies of the three occupying powers, and 450,000 lost their lives.

Despite the terrible toll, an independent Poland rose from the ashes of war in November 1918. For the first time in 123 years, Poland appeared on maps of Europe.

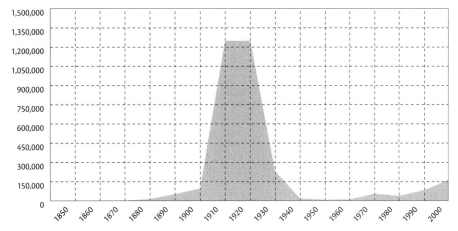

Note: *Immigration figures from 1901 to 1920 are estimates.*

The United States Closes Its Doors

During World War I, Polish Americans had fought bravely in the American armed forces. They also supported the United States on the home front.

Despite the patriotic efforts of Poles and other immigrant groups, however, American politicians were strongly against immigration after the war. In Europe the war had left an enormous population of refugees who sought entrance into the United States. In addition, political turmoil in Russia had created fear that immigrants would bring political upheaval with them to the United States. These factors led to the widespread public approval of anti-immigrant laws in the 1920s. The leaders in support of these laws were the men who had organized the Immigration Restriction League.

The rise in influence of the IRL came after years of pressure. As World War I came to an end, the IRL was finally able to force through the immigration law it had long sought. Passed over the veto of President Woodrow Wilson in 1917 by a vote in Congress, the literacy law required all adult immigrants to be literate in their native language. In families, only the husband was required to be literate.

In reality, the law did little to keep out immigrants. By the time it was passed, most European countries had higher literacy rates than they had in 1895, when the IRL was founded and started pushing for the law. Of the 800,000 immigrants who came to the United States between 1920 and 1921, only 1,450 were barred because they failed the test. For Poles, whose literacy rate was nearly 70 percent (meaning that 70 percent of them could read and write), the law had little effect.

*This is the passport of an immigrant who came to the United States
from Poland via Buenos Aries, with his wife in 1921.*

Nevertheless, the IRL's relentless pressure had caused strong anti-immigrant sentiment to arise in the United States. In response, Congress passed a quota plan in 1921 to limit the number of immigrants entering the United States. Under the quota, only a certain number of immigrants from each country or ethnic group were allowed into the United States each year. This quota virtually closed the door to Poles as it did to other immigrant groups.

Yet even these quotas were not strict enough for many Americans at the time. These nativists, as they were known, including the IRL, wanted to reduce even further the numbers of immigrants allowed into the United States.

The Immigration Act of 1924 was the result. It lowered the percentage of immigrants allowed into the United States from Europe to 2 percent of the European population already in the United States. But instead of using the population figures from the most recent census in 1920, Congress based the quota on the 1890 census. In 1890, there were far fewer immigrants from eastern and southern Europe, including Poles, than there were in 1920. Basing the new quota on the population in 1890 meant that only a very small number of immigrants from these areas would be allowed into the United States each year. Under the 1924 act, only about 5,000 Poles were allowed to immigrate to the United States each year.

"Industrious . . . Frugal . . . Loyal"

On April 8, 1924, Robert H. Clancy, a congressional representative from Detroit whose district served a large number of immigrants, attacked the new immigration bill in Congress, calling it "un-American." The Immigration Act was particularly unfair to Poles and other eastern European immigrants. In his speech, Clancy singled out the Poles in his district for special praise:

The Polish-Americans are as industrious and as frugal and as loyal to our institutions as any class of people who have come to the shores of this country in the past 300 years. They are essentially home builders, and they have come to this country to stay. They learn the English language as quickly as possible, and take pride in the rapidity with which they become assimilated and adopt our institutions.

With the entry of new immigrants virtually prohibited, the 1920s saw Polish Americans develop in two directions. In one way, the Polish-American communities in the United States became more closely knit, with the establishment of community self-help organizations and influential Catholic parishes. On the other hand, many Poles attempted to become more assimilated, or blended, into American life.

Whether they sought to hold onto their culture or become more Americanized, Poles were alike in one way: They were joiners. By 1920, there were more than 7,000 Polish organizations in the United States. More than two-thirds of all Polish Americans belonged to one or more of these societies, clubs, or foundations. The two largest such groups were the Polish National Alliance (PNA) and the Polish Roman Catholic Union (PRCU). For a long time, the primary debate between the two groups centered on what sort of independent Poland each favored. The PNA favored a democracy modeled on the United States. The PRCU wanted a democracy under a religious leader from the Catholic Church.

During the 1920s, however, few American Poles chose to return to the new homeland. Only about 10,000 out of a population of 2.5 million Polish Americans left the United States for Poland. Even so, Polish Americans supported their homeland. The PNA and PRCU were joined during the decade by other Polish societies in efforts to collect money for the struggling nation.

Although the PNA and PRCU were national Polish organizations, one of the hallmarks of Polish communities in the United States was their focus on local issues. Religious societies within church parishes often developed into nonreligious groups that organized everything from cultural events to local sports teams.

The most widely supported neighborhood organizations, however, were building-and-loan services. Most of these services operated like community-run banks. Members of the building-and-loan societies contributed small amounts of cash from time to time. When members wished to purchase a home or property, they had the right to take out loans from the community bank.

Unlike regular banks, which often denied credit and loans to immigrants, these organizations guaranteed to their members that money would generally be available to borrow. This type of community organization was not unique to Poles, but the Polish-run building-and-loan organizations were widely considered the most successful.

Like many other immigrant groups during a period when immigration was limited, Poles in the United States began to disagree about what it meant to be Polish American. Reflecting the opposing ideals of the PNA and the PRCU, Polish Americans debated whether they should speak English or Polish at home and whether they should marry non-Poles and non-Catholics. As with many questions concerning Polish identity, the church played a large role in these disagreements.

The devotion of Poles to their churches gave rise to parochial (church-run) schools in Polish neighborhoods. In 1921, there were 521 parochial schools in the 762 parishes in Polish-American communities throughout the United States. In all, these schools taught more than two-thirds of all Polish-American children. While regular classes were taught in English, religious instruction was

It's a Fact!

Polish Americans gave so much money to their churches during the 1920s that estimates place the total wealth of these churches at about $100 million at that time. Remarkably, in today's money, this equals just over $1 billion.

conducted in Polish. For the supporters of the PRCU, these schools were an ideal setting to pass on traditional Catholic Polish beliefs. For those who supported the PNA point of view, however, parochial schools became a "barrier to assimilation." In fact, many parochial schools encouraged the assimilation of Polish immigrants. Catholic leaders knew that assimilation would make Americans of other ethnicities more likely to accept both Polish Americans and the Catholic Church as well.

Assimilation did progress throughout the 1920s. For the first time, Polish newspapers, which numbered more than 150, began to publish sections in English. The papers were delivered not only to homes but to community centers, called Dom Polski (Polish Home). These halls, found in the largest Polish-American communities, were built by PNA supporters. They had auditoriums for speakers and cultural events as well as libraries where even nonreaders could have sections of the newspaper read to them in either Polish or English.

While the 1920s saw the spread of English into Polish communities, the expanding American economy played an even greater role in helping some Poles assimilate. People with money could spend it on modern inventions such as radios, motion pictures, and automobiles, which came into widespread use at the time. Not only could Polish Americans hear and see the world outside

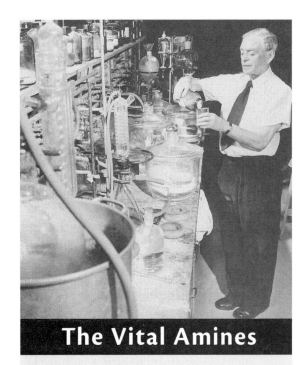

The Vital Amines

Casimir Funk was born in Warsaw, Poland, in 1884. After earning a degree in chemistry, Funk came to the United States in 1915.

In his research, Funk found that a chemical known as an amine cured the tropical disease beriberi. He suggested that certain diseases could be prevented by eating foods that contain "vital amines." In 1922, he combined "vital amines" into one word and used it as the title of an important book about his research, *The Vitamines*. Today, "vital amines" are known as vitamins. Funk's work blazed the trail toward the creation of the vitamin supplements that many people take today.

of their communities, they could travel to other areas as well. A study of Poles in Buffalo, New York, in the 1920s found that those who bought modern consumer goods almost always abandoned their ethnic traditions and sought to move from working-class neighborhoods to the suburbs.

The Depression

When the Immigration Act of 1924 was passed, it ended an era of more than 40 years of heavy immigration to the United States. The flood of newcomers to America was reduced to a trickle. But the Great Depression, a period during which the U.S. economy collapsed, brought even more changes to the pattern of immigration to the United States. The depression began in 1929. By early 1930, businesses and banks across the country had failed. By 1932, one of every four American workers was jobless. This was one of the darkest eras in American history.

For the first five years of the 1930s, the number of people leaving the United States was greater than the number of people entering the country. For the entire 10-year period from 1930 to 1940, a total of 69,000 immigrants came to the United States, an average of 6,900 per year. This was a dramatic decrease. In 1914, more people than that had entered the country every two days.

All Americans suffered during the depression, and immigrants were among those who suffered most. Industrial workers, whose ranks included large numbers of Polish Americans, were particularly hard hit by the economic disaster. Because of it, their assimilation into mainstream society was suddenly blocked. Only a few years before, Polish Americans had been moving out of working-class neighborhoods and buying larger pieces of property. Now they were mostly jobless and their options were limited.

Competition for what few jobs there were created ill will among various ethnic groups. Bad feelings arose as employers played one group off another for sought-after work. This led to a rise in the use of ethnic slurs—cruel, insulting names based on a group's ethnicity—among immigrants that grew worse as the depression wore on.

One Clergyman's Contribution

One of the most popular figures who helped to balance the traditional Polish culture with modern American society was a Catholic clergyman from New Britain, Connecticut, named Father Lucian Bojnowski. Bojnowski was born in Poland and emigrated to the United States in 1888. After he became a priest in 1895, he was assigned to the Sacred Heart Parish in New Britain, Connecticut. For the next 65 years, Bojnowski built Sacred Heart into one of the largest and most influential Polish congregations in the United States.

Bojnowski understood from the beginning of his service that his parishioners would be caught between two cultures. His goal was to keep them proud of their Polish culture even as they entered American society. The parochial school under his direction taught classes in both Polish and English. All students had to take a course in Polish history. He founded the most successful Polish language newspaper in Connecticut and helped recruit soldiers during World War I.

Bojnowski's role in the community earned him national and international fame. This brought thousands of immigrants to the industrial city of New Britain, which today still has one of the largest Polish communities in the United States.

In Chicago, which then had the largest Polish population in the world outside of Warsaw, Polish Americans lived in crowded apartments in the north end of the city. One Polish neighborhood was known as Pullman, named for the Pullman Railroad car factory, at which most of the neighborhood's residents worked. Jeffrey Dybek, whose grandfather had immigrated from Poland in 1913, recalls growing up in the Pullman neighborhood during the depression. At that time, the Pullman plant was laying off workers and unemployment was part of daily life.

Dybek describes his grandfather, Jacob, as "a [grouchy] old man, who could speak Russian, Italian, German, and Polish fluently." Jacob's ability with languages helped him find a job working in the post office in the Pullman neighborhood after losing his factory job. Jeffrey Dybek also remembers the apartment in which he grew up, one floor above his grandparents. "It was too small for five brothers and my mother and father," he says. "There was no bathtub or hot water. We had to use a wash bucket for bathing and laundry. Gas was the source of heat and light in the three rooms. The only plumbing was one sink and a toilet. The five of us children shared one bedroom which was really one half of the kitchen divided off by curtains," Dybek recalls.

Like many immigrant groups, Polish Americans depended on aid programs of the federal government to help them through the difficult days of the depression. Because they were primarily industrial workers, many immigrants, including Polish Americans, were unemployed for much of the decade. By the end of the 1930s, however, events in their faraway homeland would result in a massive reemployment of industrial workers in the United States. World War II, which would cause death and destruction in Europe, also created new opportunities for Polish Americans and other immigrants.

Opposite: *Taken in 1946, the year after World War II ended, this photograph shows the devastation suffered by Warsaw, Poland's capital city, as a result of the war. Poland's population was devastated along with its cities.*

Chapter Five

War and Communism

Poland in Turmoil

Hitler and Stalin

Throughout the 1930s, while the United States and much of the industrialized world suffered through the Great Depression, war once again threatened Europe. And as it had been throughout its long history, Poland was trapped between two powerful militaristic nations. To the west was Nazi Germany under the control of Adolf Hitler. To the east lay the Soviet Union, a nation born in the Russian Revolution of 1917, which was controlled by Joseph Stalin.

Hitler and Stalin are regarded as two of the most brutal tyrants in history. Both men had risen to power by focusing attention on their nations' so-called enemies. For Stalin, enemies were people who did not support his style of communism, the system of government that had been set up in 1917. For Hitler, the enemies were mostly Jews.

During the last half of the 1930s, Hitler's armies invaded countries beyond Germany's borders, such as Czechoslovakia and Austria. Stalin felt that he could do the same and gain some territory in Poland. This would be an initial step in spreading his Communist government around the world. Thus, while Poland struggled to achieve a democratic government, two of the worst mass murderers in history made secret deals to conquer and divide the country yet again.

In August 1939, Stalin and Hitler signed a secret agreement that would divide Poland between their two countries. Stalin,

It's a Fact!

The actions of Germany and the Soviet Union during World War II forced Poles to endure some of the worst wartime conditions in modern European history. The Nazis forced about 2 million Poles into slave labor camps. The Soviets forcibly sent nearly 1.7 million Poles to work camps in the Arctic province of Siberia.

however, planned to wait until Hitler's forces were far away, then march across Poland and attack Germany. Hitler also had no intention of honoring the agreement with Stalin. Once his own forces invaded Poland, he intended to send them all the way to Moscow, the Soviet Union's capital city.

World War II Begins

On August 22, 1939, as Nazi armed forces were gathering at the Polish border, Hitler authorized his commanders to kill "without pity or mercy, all men, women, and children of Polish descent or language. Only in this way can we obtain the living space we need." On September 1, 1939, Nazi Germany invaded Poland and conquered the western half of the nation within several weeks. This invasion marked the beginning of World War II, the most devastating period in the history of Poland.

Across Poland, as the Germans invaded from the west and the Soviets took over from the east, innocent men, women, and children were forced from their homes with no warning. They were loaded into railway cars normally used for cattle and transported either to German camps or Soviet camps. Regardless of where they were being sent, many Poles died in the filthy, freezing cars.

Until the spring of 1941, Nazi Germany and the Soviet Union maintained peaceful relations while both powers brutalized the Poles. But that June, Germany pushed through eastern Poland and invaded the Soviet Union. The effect of this was that the Poles suffered at the hands of both the retreating Soviet army and the invading German forces. By summer, all of Poland was under Nazi control.

Hitler considered Poland an important part of his German empire because of its fertile farmlands and extensive system of railway lines. The first step in controlling Poland, according to Hitler and his Nazi supporters, was to eliminate not only rebellious Poles, but all Jews in the country. Because Poland had been a relatively tolerant kingdom early in its history, the country had become the home of the largest population of Jews in Europe. Thus Poland became the starting point for Hitler's intended "Final Solution," which was the total extermination of all Jews. Today this is known as the Holocaust.

Death camps such as Auschwitz, Majdanek, Treblinka, and Sobibor operated on Polish soil. In these camps, Nazis gassed and cremated nearly all of Poland's 3 million Jews.

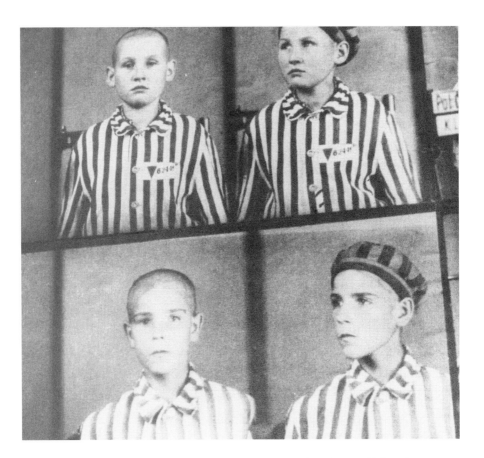

Children prisoners at the Nazi death camp at Auschwitz, Poland, were photographed in January 1945 when Soviet troops liberated the camp.

The first death camps began operation in late 1941, at the same time that other key events occurred in the war. On December 7, 1941, the Japanese launched a surprise attack against the United States at Pearl Harbor, Hawaii. On December 8, the United States declared war on Japan, which had formed an alliance with Hitler's Germany and the nation of Italy. On December 11, these countries, known as the Axis powers, declared war on the United States.

At first the Axis powers had the upper hand. But as the year wore on, the Allied powers, which included the United States and the Soviet Union, began to achieve military success.

By mid-1943, Soviet forces were pushing the Nazis back across Poland. But as the war turned in favor of the Allies, the Soviet shadow over Poland and eastern Europe began to loom larger. In 1945, Soviet forces entered Warsaw and took control. A new, unelected Polish Communist government supported by the Soviet Union was put in power.

> ## It's a Fact!
>
> **Thousands of Polish-American men of military age volunteered for the U.S. armed services to fight in World War II. Other Polish Americans, including men who were above military age as well as women, worked in manufacturing jobs to turn out the weapons and other supplies needed to fight the war.**

Polish Americans Organize

As it became clear to Polish Americans that the Soviet Union intended to take over Poland, they expressed the hope that Allied leaders, including U.S. president Franklin Roosevelt, would insist that the Soviets withdraw from Polish territory. To advance their cause, more than 2,500 representatives of Polish-American organizations across the United States met in Buffalo, New York, in late 1944. There, they founded the Polish American Council (PAC), which became—and still remains—the largest Polish-American political interest group in the United States. Charles Rozmarek, the first president of the PAC, described the two major goals of the new organization. First, the PAC wanted to "cooperate to the fullest extent with our government in order to hasten . . . the victory for . . . America and her Allies." Second and, in some ways, more important, the PAC warned the Allies that the Soviet Union must be prevented from absorbing Poland into its empire.

The Cold War

At the end of World War II, the Soviet Union, an Allied power, controlled most of eastern Europe, including Poland. In a speech in 1946, Soviet leader Joseph Stalin declared that democratic nations could never live side by side with nations such as his that were ruled by communism—a political system in which there is no private property. Around the same time, a U.S. official in Moscow wrote a memo in which he called communism a danger to the free world. It was now clear that the communism of the Soviet Union and the democracy of the United States, two vastly different systems of government, were in conflict. This conflict became known as the *cold war*. The term *cold war* referred to a conflict between large, powerful nations that involved political tension but not all-out war. The cold war would last for decades until the 1980s, when a small group of workers in a Polish shipyard began a movement that eventually brought about the fall of communism in Europe and the Soviet Union.

But the Allied powers did nothing to protect Poland from the Soviet Union. Although Poland remained on the map of Europe, it was little more than a colony of the Soviet Union. Under Stalin's iron-fisted rule, Poland and other Soviet-occupied countries in eastern Europe were tied to the Soviet Union. If any group of Poles or those from any of the other satellite nations threatened the Communists by attempting to regain control of their homelands, the Soviet-picked governments in those countries called on their own armies or secret police to stamp out dissent. If that did not work, those governments could call on the Soviet army itself

Poles in Poland and the United States were infuriated. Polish citizens were forced to watch as Soviets marched in triumph through Warsaw, celebrating not only their victory over the Nazis, which came in the spring of 1945, but also their possession of the fertile lands of Poland.

The Soviet occupation of Poland began an entirely new stage in Polish history. With a Communist-dominated government, Poland became a country modeled on the Soviet Union.

In 1948, as Stalin's move to spread communism across Europe presented a crisis to democratic nations, U.S. president Harry Truman requested that Congress pass the Displaced Persons Act. This law would allow some European refugees, including Poles, to immigrate to the United States despite the quota restrictions passed in 1924. Many of the new immigrants who came as a result of the Displaced Persons Act were orphans whose parents had been killed in the war. Others were refugees left homeless by the war who had relatives in the United States.

The Polish American Congress was very active in bringing Polish refugees to the United States. In 1948, PAC support for the Displaced Persons Act played a key role in its passage. At the same time, PAC struggled for recognition as a serious force on the American political scene. Its main goal was to change the U.S. immigration laws. While the Displaced Persons Act allowed several thousand Poles to immigrate to the United States, the quotas for Polish immigrants remained the same as they had been in 1924–slightly more than 5,000 Poles per year.

To make matters worse, in 1952 Congress passed the McCarren-Walter Act, which kept the same quotas but made immigration from eastern and central Europe even more difficult. At this period, many Americans feared that Communists were working to take over the U.S. government. In addition, many Americans and lawmakers feared that some immigrants attempting to enter the United States might be Communist spies. Restricting immigration from Communist-controlled countries therefore seemed to make sense. As a result, the McCarren-Walter Act was passed by Congress over President Truman's veto.

Change for Polish Americans

The combination of the McCarren-Walter Act and strict Soviet laws that prevented Poles from traveling outside of Communist nations greatly diminished Polish immigration. From 1946 until 1960, only about 17,000 Poles immigrated to the United States, slightly more than 1,000 immigrants per year.

While Polish ethnic communities remained close-knit, the lack of newcomers meant that fewer and fewer Polish Americans spoke their native language. Studies showed that more than 6 million Polish Americans were living in the United States in the late 1940s. Of that number, fewer than 900,000 were fluent in Polish.

Young Polish Americans, many dressed in traditional costumes, took part in a parade in April 1948 in New York City to raise money for starving children in postwar Europe.

An example of the changes that occurred in Polish-American communities after World War II can be found in the story of Hamtramck, Michigan, an industrial city east of Detroit. The rise of the automobile industry in the early 1900s drew enormous numbers of workers of all ethnic groups to the city, but by 1924, Hamtramck's population was almost 50 percent Polish. Throughout the 1930s and 1940s, public schools in Hamtramck, reflecting the immigrant population, were named after famous Poles, such as American Revolutionary War heroes

Tadeusz Kosciuszko and Kazimierz Pulaski and astronomer Nicolaus Copernicus. School libraries and the Hamtramck Public Library offered many Polish publications. Cultural presentations in the schools always included Polish traditions. Hamtramck parochial schools taught classes in Polish history, language, and literature. There were also bilingual classes (taught in both Polish and English) in subjects such as math and social studies. Report cards were written in Polish.

Polish Falcons of America

In addition to mutual aid societies, Polish immigrants organized clubs that emphasized sports and fitness. One such club was the Polish Falcons of America. This group encouraged its members to become physically fit through exercise and military drills. They established clubs in Polish communities throughout the East and Midwest where they helped maintain parks and other sports facilities. Many Polish Americans who fought in World War I and World War II were Falcons who entered military service in prime physical shape.

But by the late 1940s, change was coming to Hamtramck, as it was elsewhere in American Polonia. Second- and third-generation Polish Americans, whose parents and grandparents had immigrated from Europe, were not teaching their children the Polish language or using it at home. Between 1940 and 1965, about 20 percent of Polish-American children spoke Polish. By 1969, less than 10 percent of all Polish Americans could speak the language.

Opposite: *These Polish Americans, named queen and king of a Minnesota polka festival in 1990, show pride in their Polish heritage.*

Chapter Six

Postwar Polish Americans

Assimilation Continues

After the War

Although Polish Americans found greater economic opportunity in the decades following World War II, most remained at a level of society considered lower middle-class. Before World War II, the need for all members of Polish families to work to support the family often meant that education for young Polish Americans ended in high school. Fewer than 15 percent attended college during the two decades after World War II. More than 30 percent of Polish Americans were classified as unskilled laborers and fewer than 25 percent had so-called white-collar jobs in business, banking, or other fields that required a college education.

Nevertheless, for Polish Americans, the years from 1950 to 1970 were a time of continued assimilation into mainstream American society. Polish Americans entered fields such as professional sports, entertainment, and politics.

Sports and Entertainment

In sports, the 1950s were the glory years of Stan Musial, a Major League Baseball outfielder for the St. Louis Cardinals. Polish American "Stan the Man," as Musial was known, is widely considered one the top 10 players in baseball history. The 1950s also saw the growth of professional football. National Football League (NFL) teams were first formed in northern industrial cities such as Chicago, Cleveland, and Pittsburgh. Those teams, the Bears, Browns, and Steelers, had many Polish-American players. The Pro Football Hall of Fame, in fact, includes many Polish-American players, such as Frank Gatski, Ray Nitschke, Chuck Bednarik, Alex Wojciechowicz, and Bronco Nagurski.

Each of these Polish-American players helped to make professional football the enormously popular sport it has become.

The world of entertainment also drew Polish Americans. In the 1950s one of the most popular entertainers of all was Wladislaw Liberace, known to most people simply as Liberace. The son of an Italian father and a Polish mother, Liberace was a classically trained pianist who played concerts before thousands of music fans in the 1950s.

Wladislaw Liberace is pictured as a young man. Born in 1919, Liberace, a pianist, had become one of the most popular entertainers in the United States by the 1950s. He died in 1987.

Despite successes in sports and entertainment, a negative stereotype, or commonly held perception, that Polish Americans were uneducated, violent, and less intelligent than other people was reinforced by some aspects of American culture. In 1950, for example, the award-winning playwright Tennessee Williams received wide acclaim for his play *A Streetcar Named Desire.* The work first became a Broadway hit and then one of the most popular movies of the period, mostly due to the acting of a young star named Marlon Brando. Brando played the main character of the drama, a brutal Polish-American alcoholic named Stanley Kowalski. In the play Kowalski constantly argues with his sister-in-law, Blanche DuBois, who uses ethnic slurs to refer to Kowalski's Polish background. Williams's creation of Kowalski, coupled with the facts that most Polish Americans were employed in manufacturing jobs and not college educated, added to the unfair stereotypes of Polish Americans.

Polka Music

One of the most significant ways in which the Polish-American community reached out to American society at large during the 1950s, 1960s, and 1970s was through polka music. This style of music, clearly identified with Polish Americans and associated with traditional polka dancing, provided more than simply popular entertainment. It was also a method of communication.

The most famous polka artists came from Chicago and included Gene Wisniewski and Frank Wojnarowski. Later the Chicago tradition of polka was carried on by musicians Marion Lush and Eddie Blazonczyk. These artists used their music to demonstrate the patriotism of Polish Americans during the 1950s and 1960s. As was the case with many ethnic groups for much of the 20th century, nativists questioned whether Polish Americans were more Polish than American. Polka music helped to bridge the divide. Many polka shows closed with patriotic tunes such as "God Bless America" and "The Star-Spangled Banner." This symbolized for Poles and others who enjoyed the music the loyalty of Polish Americans to their adopted homeland.

Polka performers also played songs that touched on issues important to the Polish-American community. For example, Marion Lush's "I'll Build You a Home" spoke to the Polish Americans' strong belief in property ownership. Other polkas, such as "The Coal-Miner's Oberek" (waltz) and "Iron Foundry Polka," honored the lives of working-class Polish Americans.

Speaking Polish

A number of words commonly used in English originated in Poland or are taken directly from the Polish language.

babka: a type of coffee cake

horde: a teeming crowd of people

kielbasa: a spicy sausage

pierogi: small dumplings or pies stuffed with cabbage, cheese, or potato

polka: Polish folk dance and music

Polkas also asserted ethnic pride. "Love and Peace," a polka by Happy Louis, was sung in English. The song's lyrics tell listeners, "Let's cut out those Polish jokes / We're as good as other folks." The chorus repeats, "Stop those Polish jokes / And love those Polish folks." The lyrics also name Polish heroes of the past, such as Tadeusz Kosciuszko and Kazimierz Pulaski. Just as American music in general—including rock and roll, folk, and country—gave voice to social change in the middle decades of the 20th century, polka music communicated Polish feelings to non-Polish Americans and gained positive recognition for the Polish-American community.

Politics, Education, and Business

Polish Americans also achieved notable success in American politics, education, and business in the 1950s, 1960s, and 1970s. In addition, political successes were achieved by Polish Americans in the decades after World War II mainly through organizations and efforts in Polish-American communities in the United States. Polish Americans were also instrumental in promoting anti-Soviet efforts in their homeland.

Throughout their history as an immigrant group, Poles had been strongly supportive of local organizations. These groups were partly social clubs, but they also worked to improve local neighborhoods and help new immigrants adjust to American society. Although many other immigrant groups also had community organizations, they began to decline in membership as the immigrants assimilated into mainstream society. This was not the case for Polish Americans. In 1950, more than three-fourths of all Polish-American adults belonged to a Polish society. In Chicago alone, there were more than 4,000 Polish societies that sponsored cultural events, lectures, and festivals. They also supported Polish causes of all kinds.

The primary focus of many Polish societies in the 1950s was to encourage efforts by those still in their homeland to oppose the Communist rule of Poland. After several years of Soviet control, the Polish Communist leadership had become almost an exact copy of the so-called Stalinist Soviets. Poland was a nation of strictly controlled news, secret police, failing industries, and harassment of Catholics, since the Soviets were against religion of any kind.

While many of the political efforts of Polish Americans were directed toward their homeland, some Polish Americans did enter the American political mainstream. In 1955, Polish American Edmund Muskie became the governor of Maine. In 1958, Muskie became the first Polish American elected to the U.S. Senate. Muskie went on to win reelection for three terms. In 1968, Muskie was the Democratic vice presidential candidate, and he completed his career in government service as the secretary of state under President Jimmy Carter, who was in office from 1977 to 1981.

During the 1950s, one of the strongest anti-Communist voices on the American educational scene was Harvard University professor Zbigniew Brzezinski. Brzezinski was born in Warsaw and came to the

Zbigniew Brzezinski, shown here in 1979, was national security advisor under President Jimmy Carter.

United States in 1950. During the 1960s he served as an adviser to Presidents John Kennedy and Lyndon Johnson. His leadership was important in the move to get the U.S. government to balance an aggressive policy against the leaders of the Soviet Union with an effort to open relations with eastern European nations such as Poland, whose citizens wanted democracy. In 1977, President Jimmy Carter appointed Brzezinski to the position of national security adviser.

The growing U.S. economy after World War II presented opportunities for Polish Americans that had not been available to them before the 1940s. For decades, jobs in manufacturing, primarily in northern industrial cities, had offered steady employment to Polish Americans. But now the common American dream of becoming a self-made business owner was also within reach of many Polish Americans. One of the most successful examples was Polish-American business owner Edward Piszek. In 1946, with an investment of $350, Piszek founded a company called Mrs. Paul's that produced frozen fish sticks, which became one of the most popular foods in American homes over the following decades. By the end of the 1950s, Piszek was worth more than $100 million.

Once he became financially successful, Piszek devoted most of his time to helping Poles in Poland and standing up against the Polish stereotypes that had become common by that time. In the 1960s, Piszek bought and shipped equipment to Poland to fight the disease tuberculosis (TB), which devastated the country during the 1960s. Through those efforts, he met and became close friends with a Polish Catholic cardinal, Karol Wojtyla, who would later become known to the world as Pope John Paul II. When Poland suffered food shortages in the 1970s and 1980s, Piszek donated more than 10 million pounds of food. He also funded a corps of young people that traveled to Poland to teach English.

Throughout his life, Piszek spoke out strongly against the Polish stereotypes that appeared in the American media. In 1971, in an effort to show the rich contributions that Poles had made throughout history, he founded the Copernican Society in Chicago. Named after the Pole Nicolaus Copernicus, the "father of modern astronomy," the society has become one the most successful Polish-American organizations in the country, sponsoring cultural events, festivals, English classes, citizenship classes, and many other public services.

Immigration and the Fall of Communism

In 1965, after years of pressure from Polish Americans and other immigrant groups, Congress passed the Immigration Act of 1965, which was signed into law by President Lyndon Johnson. Under the act, 120,000 immigrants were allowed into the United States each year from nations in the Western Hemisphere (North America, South America, and Central America). Another 170,000 were allowed from all other nations, but not more than 20,000 of these immigrants could come from any single country. Immigrants with family members already in the United States, educated workers, and refugees were given highest priority.

In effect, the 1965 law ended the quota system begun in 1921. It also allowed a greater number of Poles to come to the United States. Between 1965 and 1970, about 53,500 Poles immigrated to the United States. This was three times the number of immigrants that had come in the previous 20 years. As this new wave of Poles came to the United States, Poland itself began a long and painful decade of change.

In 1970, Polish workers organized huge strikes to protest price increases on basic government-supplied goods such as bread and soap. The Polish government declared the peaceful protests unlawful and ordered the military to use deadly force against the workers. Troops killed hundreds of protesters and permanently embittered millions of Poles.

Greenpoint, Brooklyn

The Greenpoint section of Brooklyn, New York, is known for its many churches, row houses, and small shops. This neighborhood also has one of the largest concentrations of Polish immigrants in the United States. Polish immigrants first settled in Greenpoint in the early 1900s because it was close to the factories of New York City. As more Polish immigrants arrived, the neighborhood became a haven for Poles who wanted to live near others from the old country. Even today, you can hear Polish spoken on the streets of Greenpoint. Many of the shops and restaurants sell traditional Polish foods and other Polish goods. Polish community centers in Greenpoint still help new arrivals from Poland find their way in their new country.

The anti-Communist feelings increased enormously in 1978 when the archbishop of Kraków, Cardinal Karol Wojtyla, was selected to lead the world's Catholics as Pope John Paul II. Wojtyla was the first non-Italian pope in 400 years, and his election as pope united Poles in the United States and Poland as no other event had. In his role as pope, John Paul immediately spoke out forcefully against communism. He visited Poland as pope in 1979, a visit that is largely acknowledged as the beginning of the end for Polish communism.

Opposite: *Polish immigrant Evita Ciezarek was crowned Miss Polonia California 2003 in Los Angeles. Women with at least one parent born in Poland may enter the contest which celebrates Polish heritage.*

Chapter Seven

Modern Polonia

1980–Today

*Most Polish immigrants have settled
in these states.*

Solidarity

Beginning in 1980, enormous political and economic
upheaval in Poland created a new wave of immigration to
the United States. While Poland was under tight Communist
control in the 1970s, only about 37,000 immigrants came to the
United States. In the 1980s, however, as Poland made the often
painful change to democracy and faced economic difficulties,
more than 97,000 Poles came to the United States.

By 1980, workers' protests and the anti-Communist
speeches of Pope John Paul II and other Polish Catholic leaders

had created a rebellious atmosphere in Poland. At the same time, the failing policies of the Communist government were creating an economic depression across eastern Europe. In Gdansk, a group known as Solidarity demanded a greater voice for workers in government and insisted on the right to form a labor union free from government control. With growing popular support, the Solidarity workers went on strike until the government agreed to allow a nationwide union.

The Solidarity movement soon had more than 10 million members, which was more than one of every four Poles. In the United States, Polish-American organizations contributed large amounts of food, clothing, and money to the anti-Communist movement. Leading the efforts in the United States was the Polish American Congress (PAC). The PAC supported the Solidarity union and publicly criticized the Polish Communist government. At the same time, the PAC Charitable Foundation was formed. In 1981, the foundation sent more than $80,000 in medical supplies and other equipment to Poland.

Solidarity soon became a threat not only to the Communist leaders of Poland, but to the entire Soviet system. In December 1981, the military dictator of Poland ordered the army and special police units to seize control of the country, arrest Solidarity's leaders, and prevent all further union activity. In addition, the government imposed severe limits on personal and religious freedoms. Throughout 1982, as the Polish-American community—and the world—watched with alarm, the Polish Communists undid much of Solidarity's work and eventually disbanded the union.

Communist leaders soon found out, however, that they had not destroyed Solidarity. Supported in part by donations from Polish Americans, Solidarity members operated in secret or from their jail cells. In the summer of 1983, the situation worsened for the Communist government. Catholic Church leaders discovered that secret police had kidnapped and murdered Father Jerzy Popieluszko, a priest who was well known as the spiritual adviser of Solidarity. As a result of this murder more people began to sympathize with the Solidarity movement. Meanwhile, the economic failure of communism had begun to spread across eastern Europe.

With the country on the verge of revolution, the government began talks with opposition groups. After several months, an agreement was reached that allowed Solidarity to offer candidates for governmental elections. In June 1989, a national election swept the Communists from Poland's government. By the end of 1989, following Poland's lead, all countries under Soviet control had renounced communism. Suddenly, Poland and all of eastern Europe had entered a new era.

During a 1981 rally supporting Solidarity, several thousand demonstrators from Chicago's Polish community carried signs in English and Polish protesting the declaration of martial law in Poland.

"Coach K"

There is a prominent Polish-American name in American sports that many people find difficult to pronounce. It belongs to the coach of the Duke University men's basketball team: Mike Krzyzewski, sometimes called "Coach K."

Mike Krzyzewski (pronounced Sha-shef-ski) was born in Chicago in 1947. His father was an elevator operator and his mother a cleaning woman. In high school, Krzyzewski was recruited to play basketball for the U.S. Military Academy at West Point, New York. He became captain of the team, and after serving in the army, he decided to become a basketball coach.

In 1980, Krzyzewski became head coach at Duke University, where he has remained ever since, building what is widely considered one of the best men's college basketball programs in the United States. Now a member of the Basketball Hall of Fame, Krzyzewski coached Duke to national championships in 1991, 1992, and 2001.

The New Wave

The turmoil in Poland and its struggle to recover economic health took a great toll on the Polish people. As a result, beginning in the early 1980s, a new wave of Polish immigration began. More than 10,000 Poles a year came to the United States in the last decades of the 20th century. In 1993 alone, more than 27,000 Poles entered the United States. This was the high point in the new wave of Polish immigration.

Many Poles in this new wave, which continues more than 20 years later, have come to the United States for the same reasons as earlier generations—for work and personal freedom. Like the first large wave of immigrants, these new arrivals from Poland have settled largely in the Chicago area and in the industrial cities of Indiana, Ohio, Pennsylvania, New York, and Connecticut.

Some of these arrivals brought their families and became permanent residents of the United States. This group typically consists of well-educated business professionals. Others came on temporary six-month working passes or as students, leaving their families in Poland.

Holding onto Polish Heritage

The Bellingham, Massachusetts, public library is a meeting place for a group of elderly Polish Americans who live in the region. The group began in 1993 as the Polish Conversation Group with 10 members. By 2004, up to 50 people were attending the meetings. The original purpose of the group was to give Polish Americans a chance to brush up on their Polish language skills, but it has grown into a more wide-ranging meeting of people who share memories and mementos of their Polish heritage.

Membership is made up primarily of Polish Americans whose parents immigrated to the United States in the early 20th century. All share a common memory of the struggles their families faced living in a country whose population did not always appreciate or understand Polish culture. "We are all children of immigrants," says group founder Jane Alen. "Life wasn't easy.

Children could be mean. If they found out you had Polish parents, you were ridiculed." Even today, say members, they sometimes face difficulties because of their ethnic background. When they go to the doctor or government offices, they say, few people can pronounce their names. "I've had trouble with that for 86 years," quips John Waszkiewicz, whose last name is pronounced Vah-SKEV-itch.

For Bertha Kogut, the meetings help her remember stories her parents told her as a child. It is also interesting, she says, to keep informed about Polish-American issues. Kogut says that participating in the group reminds her that although she sometimes felt isolated and different as a child, other Polish-Americans shared similar experiences. "We were a minority group," Kogut says, "but we come to these meetings, and we find out we were not the only ones."

Beginning with the new wave and continuing today are approximately 2,000 Polish college students who come to the United States to study each year. Many of these students belong to groups such as the Polish Student Organization (PSO) in New York City. The PSO was founded in 1991 to help Polish students from sixteen colleges in the New York City. This organization sponsors events such as dances, picnics, and other outings to help Polish students get to know one another and members of the Polish communities near their schools. In addition, it is dedicated to helping the Polish-American community learn more about opportunities for higher education for their children.

Some of those who come to the United States under temporary arrangements remain in the country illegally. In the tightly knit Polish-American communities, it is relatively easy for illegal immigrants to move about and find work without being discovered. These temporary immigrants frequently live in low-income housing, sharing rooms with other immigrants, and working at low-wage jobs in order to send money to their families in Poland. They often take jobs as laborers and housekeepers.

In the large Polish-American community of New Britain, Connecticut, many recent Polish immigrants find work through a group called the Polish Connection. Those who work for this group may come to the United States on a temporary basis, or they may have relatives in the city whom they can visit for

It's a Fact!

A Polish-American immigrant was chosen to design the memorial and other buildings on the site where the World Trade Center twin towers once stood. Daniel Libeskind came to America following World War II and studied architecture in New York. He and his architectural firm will create a building 1,776 feet tall to symbolize the year of U.S. independence and to remember the nearly 3,000 people who died at the World Trade Center on September 11, 2001.

extended periods of time. Polish Connection workers are hired to provide live-in care for elderly people in the area.

For Poles such as Frank Sierpensky, the arrangement with the Polish Connection works well. Sierpensky was unable to find even part-time work as a security guard in Poland. He came to the United States and took jobs for the Polish Connection. Because he speaks fluent English, Sierpensky can be assigned to a variety of clients. Through this arrangement, he is able to send money home while keeping his living expenses low.

A Continuing Story

The decades that separate the various waves of Polish immigrants have raised some barriers between long-time Polish Americans and new arrivals. As Polish Americans assimilated throughout the 20th century, they often married non-Poles and moved away from Polish communities, blending into American society at large. Although they identify themselves as Polish Americans, they have little or no connection with Poland or the new Polish immigrants. Despite their assimilation, many Polish Americans feel a strong attachment to their ethnic heritage. This gives them something in common with recent Polish immigrants.

In 2004, Congresswoman Nancy L. Johnson, introduced a resolution in Congress that would affect many Polish immigrants and their families. Johnson represents the fifth Congressional district in Connecticut, which includes one of the largest populations of Polish Americans in the country. Her resolution urged the Department of Homeland Security to allow Polish citizens to visit relatives and friends in the United States without having to obtain a visa. They would only have to show a valid passport to enter and leave the United States. This measure would make it much easier for people to travel to and from Poland to see family members and friends who have immigrated to America. Johnson proposed the resolution in recognition of the close ties between the United States and Poland and the contribution of Polish Americans to the history of the United States.

Martha Stewart

Another widely known Polish American was born Martha Kostyra in Nutley, New Jersey, in 1941 into a large family of Polish descent. Martha's mother taught her to cook, and her father taught her to garden. She moved to New York City in the 1960s, where she married and worked in the stock market. However, cooking and entertaining were the first loves of Martha Stewart, as she was called after her marriage.

In the 1970s, Stewart moved to Connecticut, where she began to cater weddings and parties. Soon she became so popular as a caterer that she was asked to write a book about home decorating and cooking. The book, *Entertaining*, was published in 1982 and was followed by two popular cookbooks. This marked the start of a business empire that made Martha Stewart one of the most famous and wealthy women in the United States.

The relationship between Poles and America is older than the United States itself. Yet, unlike the stories of many other groups that have not continued to immigrate in large numbers after the first waves of immigration in the late 19th and early 20th centuries, the story of Polish immigration to the United States does not appear to be finished.

Whether their ties to Poland are recent or in the distant past, the pride felt by Polish Americans is powerful. Now, while Polish Americans look back with admiration at the courage and accomplishments of early Polish Americans, they look forward to passing on these traditions to the next generation of Polonia.

Time Line of
Polish Immigration

1608   First Poles arrive in North America at Jamestown, Virginia.

1609   Poland fights the first of several wars against invading armies from Sweden, Turkey, and Russia.

1777   General Tadeusz Kosciuszko designs fortifications to protect American troops from British artillery in the important American victory at Saratoga, New York.

1778   Kosciuszko designs fort overlooking the Hudson River at West Point, which becomes the U.S. Military Academy.

1779   General Kazimierz Pulaski is fatally wounded in battle at Savannah, Georgia.

1795   Russia, Prussia, and Austria partition Poland.

1854   Panna Maria, the first Polish-American community, is founded near San Antonio, Texas.

1870   U.S. Census lists 40,000 German immigrants of Polish descent in Chicago, Illinois, making it the U.S. city with the largest Polish immigrant community.

1900   Poles are listed for the first time as a separate group in the U.S. Census.

1918   World War I ends and an independent Poland is founded for the first time in 123 years.

1924   Congress passes the Immigration Act of 1924.

1939   Nazi Germany invades Poland on September 1, beginning World War II.

1941	Poland's death camps become the center of the Nazi Holocaust.
1945	Poland falls under the control of the Soviet Union and becomes a Communist state.
1948	U.S. Congress passes the Displaced Persons Act, which allows some European refugees, including Poles, to immigrate to the United States despite quotas.

1965   U.S. Congress passes the Immigration Act, which has the effect of allowing more immigrants from Poland to enter the United States each year.

1978   The archbishop of Kraków, Poland, Cardinal Karol Wojtyla, is selected to lead the Catholic Church as Pope John Paul II.

1980   Polish American Czeslaw Milosz wins the Nobel Prize for literature.

1989   National election in Poland removes Communist government and replaces it with democratic government.

2000   U.S. Census lists the population of people of Polish descent at about 9 million, ranking Poles seventh-largest among ethnic groups in the United States.

2001   Duke University men's basketball wins its third national championship under coach Mike Krzyzewski. He is inducted into the Basketball Hall of Fame.

2002   Polish Americans win a number of elections. They are Senator Chuck Hagel (NE) and Representatives Paul Kanjorski (PA), Bill Lipinski (IL), Gerald Kleczka (WI), John Dingell (MI), and Marcy Kaptur (OH). In addition, two Polish Americans become governor: Frank Murkowski (AK) and Ted Kulongoski (OR).

2004   Congresswoman Nancy Johnson of Connecticut introduces a resolution in Congress that would allow Polish citizens visiting family and friends in the United States to enter the country more easily.

Glossary

anarchist Person who is against any form of government and anyone in a position of authority.

anti-Semitism Hatred of and discrimination against Jews.

assimilate To absorb or blend into the way of life of a society.

culture The language, arts, traditions, and beliefs of a society.

democracy Government by the majority rule of the people.

emigrate To leave one's homeland to live in another country.

ethnic Having certain racial, national, tribal, religious, or cultural origins.

immigrate To come to a foreign country to live.

nativism Prejudice in favor of people born in a nation and against immigrants who settle in that nation.

parochial Having to do with a church parish, or neighborhood, such as a parochial school.

polka Polish folk dance and the music that accompanies it.

Polonia The name used by Polish Americans to refer to their ethnic group.

prejudice Negative opinion formed without just cause.

refugee Someone who flees a place for safety reasons, especially to another country.

Solidarity Group formed in Poland in the 1980s that demanded rights for workers and eventually came to power in the Polish government.

steerage Least expensive traveling class on a steamship.

stereotype Simplified and sometimes insulting opinion or image of a person or group.

Further Reading

BOOKS

Bartoletti, Susan Campbell. *A Coal Miner's Bride: The Diary of Annetka Kaminski*. New York: Scholastic, 2002.

Greene, Meg. *The Polish Americans*. San Diego: Gale Group, 2003.

Lock, Donna. *Polish Americans*. Broomall, Pa.: Mason Crest, 2002.

Moscinski, Sharon. *Tracing Our Polish Roots*. Emeryville, Calif.: Avalon Travel Publishing, 1994.

Nowakowski, Jacek. *Polish Touches: Recipes and Traditions*. Iowa City, Iowa: Penfield Press, 1996.

Wallner, Rosemary. *Polish Immigrants, 1890–1920*. Mankato, Minn.: Capstone Press, 2002.

WEB SITES

History of Poland. URL: http://www.countryreports.org/history/ polahist.htm. Downloaded on August 6, 2004.

The Immigrant Experience and the Pan-American Exposition. "The Polish Community of Buffalo and the Pan-American Exposition." URL: http://ublib.buffalo.edu/libraries/exhibits/panam/immigrants/poles. html. Downloaded on August 6, 2004.

Polish American Journal. "Preserving 'Polonia's Plymouth Rock': Panna Maria, Texas." URL: http://www.polamjournal.com/Library/ APHistory/panna/panna.html. Downloaded on August 4, 2004.

PolishRoots: The Polish Genealogy Source. "PolishRoots Surnames: Origins & Meanings." URL: http://www.polishroots.org/surnames/ surnames_endings.htm. Downloaded on August 4, 2004.

Index